The

FAIRY QUEEN

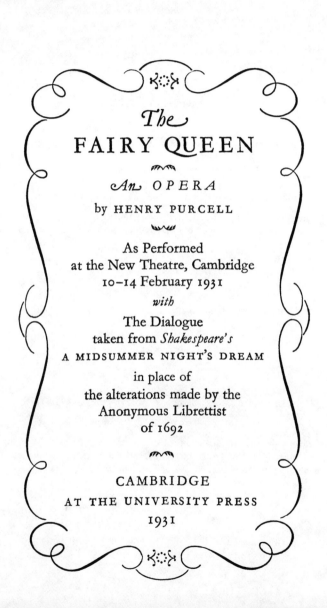

The FAIRY QUEEN

An OPERA

by HENRY PURCELL

As Performed
at the New Theatre, Cambridge
10–14 February 1931

with

The Dialogue
taken from *Shakespeare's*
A MIDSUMMER NIGHT'S DREAM

in place of
the alterations made by the
Anonymous Librettist
of 1692

CAMBRIDGE
AT THE UNIVERSITY PRESS
1931

CAMBRIDGE
UNIVERSITY PRESS

University Printing House, Cambridge CB2 8BS, United Kingdom

Published in the United States of America by Cambridge University Press, New York

Cambridge University Press is part of the University of Cambridge.

It furthers the University's mission by disseminating knowledge in the pursuit of education, learning and research at the highest international levels of excellence.

www.cambridge.org
Information on this title: www.cambridge.org/9781107634121

© Cambridge University Press 1931

First published 1931
Re-issued 2014

A catalogue record for this publication is available from the British Library

ISBN 978-1-107-63412-1 Paperback

INTRODUCTION

In the January number of the *Gentleman's Journal* of
1692 Motteux wrote:

I must tell you that we shall have speedily a New
Opera, wherein something very surprising is pro-
mised us; Mr *Purcel* who joyns to the Delicacy and
Beauty of the *Italian* way, the Graces and Gayety of
the *French*, composes the Music, as he hath done for
the *Prophetess*,[1] and the last Opera called King
Arthur, which hath been plaid several times the last
Month.

In the May number he writes:

The Opera of which I spoke to you in my former
hath at last appear'd, and continues to be represented daily; it is call'd *The Fairy Queen*. The *Drama*
is originally *Shakespears*, the *Music* and *Decorations*
are extraordinary. I have heard the Dances com-
mended, and without doubt the whole is very
entertaining.

Downes, the old prompter, is most enthusiastic
in his *Roscius Anglicanus* over the production at
Dorset Gardens Theatre, which

in Ornaments was Superior to the other Two;[2]
especially in Cloaths, for all the Singers and Dancers,

---

1 Better known as *Dioclesian*.
2 I.e. *Dioclesian* and *King Arthur*.

Scenes, Machines and Decorations, all most pro-
fusely set off; and excellently perform'd, chiefly the
Instrumental and Vocal part Compos'd by the said
Mr *Purcel*, and Dances by Mr *Priest*.[1] The Court
and Town were wonderfully satisfy'd with it; but
the Expences in setting it out being so great, the
Company got very little by it.

Among the singers were Mrs Ayliff, Mrs Dyer,
Mrs Butler (the original Philidel in *King Arthur*),
Mr Freeman, Mr Reading and Mr Pate (who sang
not only the part of Mopsa "in Woman's habit" but
that of Summer as well).

The anonymous libretto and "Some Select Songs
as they are Sung in the Fairy Queen" were published
in the same year, and a revised version "With
Alterations, Additions, and several new Songs"
appeared in 1693, in which year on Feb. 16 the
opera was attended by the Queen and "ye Maids
Honr" in two boxes.

Some more excerpts were published by Thomas
Cross and in the *Ayres for the Theatre* and *Orpheus
Britannicus*, but in the *London Gazette* for Oct. 9–13,
1701, the following advertisement appeared:

The score of the Musick for the *Fairy Queen* set by
the late Mr Henry Purcell, and belonging to the
Patentees of the Theatre Royal in Covent Garden,
London, being lost by his death, whosoever brings

[1] The ballet-master of the Opera, for whose school
Purcell had written *Dido and Aeneas*.

the said score, or a copy thereof, to Mr Zacchary Baggs, Treasurer of the said Theatre, shall have 20 guineas reward.

There was no reply to this or to a repetition of the advertisement the following week, and, but for the performance of one act of the opera at a concert on Feb. 1, 1703, by Leveridge and others and the inclusion of a couple of the tunes in *The Beggar's Opera*, little was heard of *The Fairy Queen* until two hundred years later the Purcell Society came to edit the full score for publication from several incomplete and inaccurate sources. A conjectural score was prepared and even engraved, when there was found in the library of the Royal Academy of Music a MS. volume "Op. Faire Queen" that turned out to be the missing score.

This volume, which had been bequeathed to the Royal Academy of Music in 1837 by R. J. S. Stevens (*b.* 1757), had formerly been in the possession of William Savage (*d.* 1789), who had possibly obtained it from his master Pepusch (1667–1752), an enthusiastic collector of musical manuscripts. The score had evidently been made by several copyists, who seem to have transcribed the music as Purcell wrote it, leaving blanks for what was not ready— some of which were filled up by the composer himself. From the re-discovered score the Purcell

Society Edition of the opera was edited and published in 1903.

A concert performance was given by the students of Morley College on June 10, 1911, conducted by Gustav Holst and explained by Vaughan Williams, and the first stage revival of the opera since 1693 was given at the New Theatre, Cambridge, from Feb. 10 to 14, 1920, produced by Mr Clive Carey and conducted by Dr Cyril Rootham.

The text here printed is the acting version adopted for the revival at Cambridge Feb. 10 to 14, 1931. As Prof. E. J. Dent wrote in the preface to his arrangement for the 1920 revival, "it has been thought better to restore the original text of Shakespeare as far as possible, since the alterations of Purcell's collaborator have not even the trivial merit of being amusing; but the dialogue has had to be greatly curtailed in order to bring the work within the limits of practical convenience without sacrificing Purcell's music". The present text, though it restores the *Pyramus and Thisbe* play (mimed in 1920) to its 1692 position as a rehearsal in the wood, is still further curtailed. All dialogue not essentially necessary to the action has been omitted. This entails the omission of Hippolyta, Philostrate, Peaseblossom and the other three fairies, and such famous speeches as "I know a bank". This may offend the purists, but they must be reminded that they are witnessing not *A Midsummer Night's Dream* but *The Fairy Queen*, in which Purcell's music takes the place of descriptive poetry. The original Preface and Prologue have been reprinted as throwing considerable light on the history of opera in seventeenth century England.

DENNIS ARUNDELL

1931

The PREFACE

'Tis known to all who have been any considerable time in Italy, or France, how Opera's are esteem'd among 'em. That France borrow'd what she has from Italy, is evident from the Andromede and Toison D'or, of Monsieur Corneille, which are the first in the kind they ever had, on their publick Theaters; they being not perfect Opera's, but Tragedies, with Singing, Dancing, and Machines interwoven with 'em, after the manner of an Opera. They gave 'em a tast first, to try their Palats, that they might the better Judge whether in time they would be able to digest an entire Opera. And Cardinal Richelieu (that great encourager of Arts and Learning) introduced 'em first at his own expence, as I have been informed, amongst 'em.

What encouragement Seignior Baptist Luly had from the present King of France, is well known; they being first set out at his own Expence; and all the Ornaments given by the King, for the Entertainment of the People. In Italy, especially at Venice, where Opera's have the greatest Reputation, and where they have 'em every Carnival, the Noble Venetians set 'em out at their own cost. And what a Confluence of People the fame of 'em draw from all parts of Italy to the great profit of that City, is well known to everyone who has spent a Carnival there. And many of the English Gentry are sensible what advantages Paris receives, by the great number of Strangers which frequent the Opera's three days in a Week, throughout the Year. If therefore an Opera were established here, by the Favour of the Nobility and Gentry of England; I may modestly conclude it would be some advantage to London, considering what a Sum we must Yearly lay out among Tradesmen for the fitting out so great a work.

That Sir William Davenant's Siege of Rhodes was the first Opera we ever had in England, no Man can deny; and is indeed a perfect Opera: there being this difference only between an Opera and a Tragedy; that the one is a Story sung with proper Action, the other spoken. And he must be a very ignorant Player, who knows not there is a Musical Cadence in speaking; and that a Man may as well speak out of Tune, as sing out of Tune. And though few are so nice to examine this, yet all are pleas'd when they hear it justly perform'd. 'Tis true, the Siege of Rhodes wanted the Ornament of Machines, which they Value themselves so much upon in Italy. And the Dancing which they have in such perfection in France. That he design'd this, if his

first attempt met with the Encouragement it de-
serv'd, will appear from these Lines in his Prologue.

> *But many Travellers here, as Judges, come,*
> *From Paris, Florence, Venice, and from Rome.*
> *Who will describe, when any Scene we draw,*
> *By each of ours, all that they ever saw.*
> *Those praising for extensive breadth and height,*
> *And inward distance to deceive the sight.—*

And a little after—

> *Ah Mony, Mony! if the Wits would dress*
> *With Ornaments the present face of Peace:*
> *And to our Poet half that Treasure spare,*
> *Which Faction gets from Fools to nourish War.*
> *Then his contracted Scenes should wider be,*
> *And move by greater Engines; till you see*
> *(While you securely sit) fierce Armies meet,*
> *And raging Seas disperse a fighting Fleet.*

That a few private Persons should venture on so
expensive a Work as an Opera, when none but
Princes, or States exhibit 'em abroad, I hope is no
Dishonour to our Nation: And I dare affirm if we
had half the Encouragement in England, that they
have in other Countries, you might in a short time
have as good Dancers in England as they have in
France, though I despair of ever having as good

Voices among us, as they have in Italy. These are
the two great things which Travellers say we are
most deficient in. If this happens to please, we
cannot reasonably propose to our selves any great
advantage, considering the mighty Charge in setting it out, & the extraordinary expence that attends
it every day 'tis represented. If it deserves their
Favour? if they are satisfied we venture boldly,
doing all we can to please 'em? We hope the
English are too generous not to encourage so great
an undertaking.

The PROLOGUE

What have we left untry'd to please this Age,
To bring it more in liking with the Stage?
We sunk to Farce, and rose to Comedy;
Gave you high Rants, and well-writ Tragedy.
Yet Poetry, of the Success afraid,
Call'd in her Sister Musick to her aid.
And, lest the Gallery should Diversion want,
We had Cane Chairs to Dance 'em a Courant.[1]

But that this Play may in its Pomp appear;
Pray let our Stage from thronging Beaux be clear.
For what e're cost we're at, what e're we do,
In Scenes, Dress, Dances; yet there's many a Beau,
Will think himself a much more taking Show.
How often have you curs'd these new Beau-skreens,[2]
That stand betwixt the Audience and the Scenes?

I ask'd one of 'em t'other day—Pray, Sir,
Why d'ye the Stage before the Box prefer?
He answer'd—Oh! there I Ogle the whole Theatre,
My Wig—my Shape, my Leg, I there display,
They speak much finer things than I can say.

These are the Reasons why they croud the Stage;
And make the disappointed Audience rage,
Our Business is, to study how to please,
To Tune the Mind to its expected ease.
And all that we expect, is but to find,
Equal to our Expence, the Audience kind.

1 Alluding to the Chair Dance in *Dioclesian*.
2 A reference to the new habit of the smart set sitting
on the stage.

The
NAMES *of the* PERSONS

THESEUS, *Duke of* Athens.
EGEUS, *Father to* Hermia.
LYSANDER, *in love with* Hermia.
DEMETRIUS, *in love with* Hermia, *and betrothed to* Helena.
HERMIA, *in love with* Lysander.
HELENA, *in love with* Demetrius.

THE FAIRIES

OBERON, *King of the Fairies.*
TITANIA, *the Queen.*
PUCK, *or* Robin Goodfellow.
A Fairy.

THE COMEDIANS

BOTTOM, *the weaver.*
QUINCE, *the carpenter.*
SNUG, *the joiner.*
FLUTE, *the bellows-mender.*
SNOUT, *the tinker.*
STARVELING, *the tailor.*

SINGERS & DANCERS

IN ACT I

Three Fairies.
Three drunken poets.
Chorus of Fairies.

IN ACT II

Three Fairy-Spirits.
Night ⎫
Mystery ⎟ *and their* attendants, singers *and*
Secrecy ⎬ dancers.
Sleep ⎭

IN ACT III

Three Nymphs.
Coridon.
Mopsa.
Chorus of Fauns, Dryads *and* Naiads.
Swans, Savages *and* Haymakers.

IN ACT IV

Three attendants *on the* Seasons.
Phoebus.
Spring.
Summer.
Autumn.
Winter.
Chorus and Dancers: Attendants *on the* Seasons.

xviii NAMES OF THE PERSONS

IN ACT V

JUNO.
A Chinese Man.
Chinese Women.
HYMEN.
Six Monkeys.
Chorus *and* Dance *of* Chinese.

The FAIRY QUEEN

Overture

A C T I : S C E N E I

Athens. The Palace of Theseus

Enter THESEUS, EGEUS, HERMIA, LYSANDER
and DEMETRIUS

Eg. Happy be Theseus, our renowned duke!
The. Thanks, good Egeus. What's the news with
thee?
Eg. Full of vexation come I, with complaint
Against my child, my daughter Hermia.
Stand forth, Demetrius. My noble lord,
This man hath my consent to marry her.
Stand forth, Lysander: and, my gracious duke,
This man hath bewitched the bosom of my child,
Turned her obedience, which is due to me,
To stubborn harshness: and my gracious duke,
Be it so she will not here before your grace
Consent to marry with Demetrius,

I

I beg the ancient privilege of Athens,
As she is mine, I may dispose of her.

The. What say you, Hermia? Be advised, fair
maid;
To you your father should be as a god.

Her. I do entreat your grace to pardon me.
I know not by what power I am made bold
In such a presence here to plead my thoughts;
But I beseech your grace that I may know
The worst that may befall me in this case,
If I refuse to wed Demetrius.

The. Either to die the death or to abjure
For ever the society of men,
For aye to be in shady cloister mew'd,
To live a barren sister all your life,
Chanting faint hymns to the cold fruitless moon.

Her. So will I grow, so live, so die, my lord,
Ere I will yield my virgin patent up
Unto his lordship, whose unwished yoke
My soul consents not to give sovereignty.

Dem. Relent, sweet Hermia: and, Lysander, yield
Thy crazed title to my certain right.

Lys. I am, my lord, as well derived as he,
As well possessed; my love is more than his;
My fortunes every way as fairly ranked,
And, which is more than all these boasts can be,
I am beloved of beauteous Hermia:

Demetrius, I'll avouch it to his head,
Made love to Nedar's daughter, Helena.

    The. I must confess that I have heard so much.
Demetrius come: Egeus, go with me,
I have some private schooling for you both.
For you, fair Hermia, look you arm yourself
To fit your fancies to your father's will;
Or else the law of Athens yields you up
To death, or to a vow of single life.

Air [1]

             [*Exeunt* THESEUS, EGEUS *and* DEMETRIUS
    Lys. Ay me! for aught that ever I could read,
Could ever hear by tale or history,
The course of true love never did run smooth.

    Her. If then true lovers have been ever cross'd,
It stands as a decree in destiny:
Then let us teach our trial patience,
Because it is a customary cross.

    Lys. A good persuasion: therefore hear me,
      Hermia.
I have a widow aunt, a dowager
Of great revenue, and she hath no child:
From Athens is her house remote seven leagues;
And she respects me as her only son.
There, gentle Hermia, may I marry thee;

---

1 From the *Second Music.*

And to that place the sharp Athenian law
Cannot pursue us. If thou lov'st me then,
Steal forth thy father's house tomorrow night;
And in the wood, a league without the town,
There will I stay for thee.

    Her.   My good Lysander!
I swear to thee, by Cupid's strongest bow,
In that same place thou hast appointed me,
Tomorrow truly will I meet with thee.

    Lys. Keep promise, love. Look, here comes
      Helena.

Enter HELENA

    Her. God speed fair Helena! Whither away?

    Hel. Call you me fair? That fair again unsay.
O teach me how you look; and with what art
You sway the motion of Demetrius' heart!

    Her. Take comfort: he no more shall see my face;
Lysander and myself will fly this place.

    Lys. Helen, to you our minds we will unfold:
Tomorrow night, when Phoebe doth behold
Her silver visage in the watery glass,
Decking with liquid pearl the bladed grass,
A time that lovers' flights doth still conceal,
Through Athens' gates have we devised to steal.

    Her. And in the wood, where often you and I
Upon faint primrose-beds were wont to lie,
Emptying our bosoms of their counsel sweet,

There my Lysander and myself shall meet;
And thence from Athens turn away our eyes,
To seek new friends and stranger companies.
Farewell, sweet playfellow: pray thou for us;
And good luck grant thee thy Demetrius!

                [*Exeunt* HERMIA *and* LYSANDER

  Hel. How happy some o'er other some can be!
Through Athens I am thought as fair as she.
But what of that? Demetrius thinks not so;
He will not know what all but he do know.
I will go tell him of fair Hermia's flight:
Then to the wood will he tomorrow night
Pursue her; and for this intelligence
If I have thanks, it is a dear expense.   [*Exit*

Jig[1]

SCENE II

Quince's House

Enter QUINCE, SNUG, BOTTOM, FLUTE, SNOUT
and STARVELING

  Qui. Is all our company here?
  Bot. You were best to call them generally, man
by man, according to the scrip.
  Qui. Here is the scroll of every man's name,

---

1 The *First Act Tune.*

which is thought fit, through all Athens, to play in our interlude before the duke.

Bot. First, good Peter Quince, say what the play treats on, then read the names of the actors; and so grow to a point.

Qui. Marry, our play is, "The most lamentable comedy, and most cruel death of Pyramus and Thisby".

Bot. A very good piece of work, I assure you, and a merry. Now, good Peter Quince, call forth your actors by the scroll. Masters, spread yourselves.

Qui. Answer as I call you. Nick Bottom, the weaver.

Bot. Ready. Name what part I am for, and proceed.

Qui. You, Nick Bottom, are set down for Pyramus.

Bot. What is Pyramus? A lover, or a tyrant?

Qui. A lover that kills himself most gallant for love.

Bot. That will ask some tears in the true performing of it: if I do it, let the audience look to their eyes; I will move storms, I will condole in some measure. To the rest: yet my chief humour is for a tyrant; I could play Ercles rarely, or a part to tear a cat in, to make all split.

> The raging rocks
> And shivering shocks
> Shall break the locks
>   Of prison gates;
> And Phibbus' car
> Shall shine from far
> And make and mar
>   The foolish Fates.

This was lofty! Now name the rest of the players.
This is Ercles' vein, a tyrant's vein; a lover is more
condoling.

Qui. Francis Flute, the bellows-mender.

Flu. Here, Peter Quince.

Qui. Flute, you must take Thisby on you.

Flu. What is Thisby? A wandering knight?

Qui. It is the lady that Pyramus must love.

Flu. Nay, faith, let me not play a woman; I have
a beard coming.

Qui. That's all one: you shall play it in a mask,
and you may speak as small as you will.

Bot. An I may hide my face, let me play Thisby
too. I'll speak in a monstrous little voice, "Thisne,
Thisne;" "Ah Pyramus, my lover dear! thy Thisby
dear, and lady dear!"

Qui. No, no; you must play Pyramus: and,
Flute, you Thisby.

Bot. Well, proceed.

Qui. Robin Starveling, the tailor.

Sta. Here, Peter Quince.

Qui. Robin Starveling, you must play Thisby's mother. Tom Snout, the tinker.

Sno. Here, Peter Quince.

Qui. You, Pyramus' father: myself, Thisby's father. Snug, the joiner, you, the lion's part: and, I hope, here is a play fitted.

Snu. Have you the lion's part written? Pray you, if it be, give it me, for I am slow of study.

Qui. You may do it extempore, for it is nothing but roaring.

Bot. Let me play the lion too: I will roar, that I will do any man's heart good to hear me; I will roar, that I will make the duke say, "Let him roar again, let him roar again".

Qui. You can play no part but Pyramus: for Pyramus is a sweet-faced man; a most lovely, gentleman-like man: therefore you must needs play Pyramus.

Bot. Well, I will undertake it. But, Peter Quince —There are things in this comedy of Pyramus and Thisby that will never please. First, Pyramus must draw a sword to kill himself; which the ladies cannot abide. How answer you that?

Sno. By'r lakin, a parlous fear.

Sta. I believe we must leave the killing out when all is done.

Bot. Not a whit. Write me a prologue; and let the prologue seem to say, we will do no harm with our swords, and that Pyramus is not killed indeed.

Qui. Well, we will have such a prologue.

Sno. Will not the ladies be afeard of the lion?

Sta. I fear it, I promise you.

Sno. Therefore, another prologue must tell he is not a lion.

Bot. Nay, let him name his name, and tell them plainly he is Snug the joiner.

Qui. Well, it shall be so. But there is two hard things: that is to bring moonlight into a chamber; for you know, Pyramus and Thisby meet by moonlight.

Snu. Doth the moon shine that night we play our play?

Bot. A calendar! a calendar! look in the almanack: find out moonshine, find out moonshine.

Qui. Yes, it doth shine that night.

Bot. Why, then you may leave a casement of the great chamber-window, where we play, open; and the moon may shine in at the casement.

Qui. Ay; or else one must come in with a bush of thorns and a lanthorn, and say he comes to disfigure, or to present, the person of Moonshine.

Then, there is another thing: we must have a wall in the great chamber; for Pyramus and Thisby, says the story, did talk through the chink of a wall.

Snu. You can never bring in a wall. What say you, Bottom?

Bot. Some man or other must present Wall; and let him have some plaster, or some loam, or some rough-cast about him, to signify Wall; and let him hold his fingers thus, and through that cranny shall Pyramus and Thisby whisper.

Qui. If that may be, then all is well. But, masters, here are your parts; and I am to entreat you, request you, and desire you, to con them by to-morrow night; and meet me in the palace wood, a mile without the town, by moonlight: there will we rehearse—for if we meet in the city, we shall be dogged with company, and our devices known. I pray you, fail me not.

Bot. We will meet; and there we may rehearse most obscenely and courageously. Take pains; be perfect; adieu.

Qui. At the duke's oak we meet.

Bot. Enough; hold, or cut bow-strings.

[*Exeunt*

Prelude [1]

---

[1] From the *First Music*.

SCENE III

A Wood near Athens

Enter TITANIA, *leading the* INDIAN BOY, FAIRIES *attending*

Tit. Now the glow-worm shows her light,
And twinkling stars adorn the night.
Now we glide from our abodes
To sing and revel in these woods.
Are the sentries set?

Fairy.   They are.

Tit. 'Tis well. If any mortal dare
Approach this spot of fairy ground,
Blind the wretch, then turn him round.
Pinch his arms, his thighs and shins;
Pinch, till he confess his sins.
Now my fairy quire, appear,
Sing and entertain my dear:
Describe that happiness, that peace of mind
Which lovers only in retirement find.

Two   *Come, come, come, let us leave the town,*
Fairies.   *And in some lonely place,*
          Where crowds and noise were never known,
              Resolve to spend our days.

          In pleasant shades upon the grass
              At night ourselves we'll lay;
          Our days in harmless sport shall pass,
              Thus time shall slide away.

Enter FAIRIES, *leading in three drunken* POETS,
one of them blindfolded

The Poet.	*Fill up the bowl, then—*
First Fairy and Chorus. }	*Trip it, trip it in a ring,* *Around this mortal dance and sing.*
The Poet.	*Enough, enough,* *We must play at blind-man's-buff.* *Turn me round and stand away,* *I'll catch whom I may.*
Second Fairy and Chorus. }	*About him go, so, so, so,* *Pinch the wretch from top to toe;* *Pinch him forty, forty times,* *Pinch till he confess his crimes.*
The Poet.	*Hold, you vile tormenting crew,* *I confess—*
Both Fairies.	*What, what?*
The Poet.	*I'm drunk, as I live, boys, drunk.*
Both Fairies.	*What art thou, speak?*
The Poet.	*If you will know it,* *I am a scurvy poet.*
Chorus.	*Pinch him, pinch him for his crimes,* *His nonsense and his doggrel rhymes.*
The Poet.	*Oh! oh! oh!*
Both Fairies.	*Confess more, more.*
The Poet.	*I confess I'm very poor.* *Nay, prithee, do not pinch me so,* *Good dear devil, let me go;*

And as I hope to wear the bays,
I'll write a sonnet in thy praise.

Chorus. *Drive 'em hence, away, away,*
Let 'em sleep till break of day.

[*Exeunt*[1]

ACT II

The wood by moonlight

Enter, from opposite sides, a FAIRY *and* PUCK

Puck. How now, spirit! whither wander you?
Fairy. Over hill, over dale,
  Thorough bush, thorough brier,
Over park, over pale,
  Thorough flood, thorough fire,
I do wander everywhere,
Swifter than the moon's sphere;
And I serve the fairy queen,
To dew her orbs upon the green.
Farewell, thou lob of spirits; I'll be gone:
Our queen and all her elves come here anon.
  Puck. The king doth keep his revels here tonight:
Take heed the queen come not within his sight;
For Oberon is passing fell and wrath,

---

1 The whole of this scene was added for the 1693 revival.

Because that she as her attendant hath
A lovely boy, stolen from an Indian king;
She never had so sweet a changeling.

    Fairy. Either I mistake your shape and making
        quite,
Or else you are that shrewd and knavish sprite
Call'd Robin Goodfellow.

    Puck.   Thou speak'st aright;
I am that merry wanderer of the night.
But room, fairy! Here comes Oberon.

    Fairy. And here my mistress. Would that he
        were gone!

Hornpipe [1]

Enter, from one side, OBERON, *with his train;
from the other,* TITANIA, *with hers*

    Ob. Ill met by moonlight, proud Titania.

    Tit. What, jealous Oberon! Fairies, skip hence:
I have forsworn his bed and company.

    Ob. Tarry, rash wanton: am not I thy lord?

    Tit. Then I must be thy lady: but I know
That never, since the middle summer's spring,
Met we on hill, in dale, forest or mead,
But with thy brawls thou hast disturb'd our sport.

    Ob. Do you amend it then; it lies in you:

---

1 From the *First Music*.

Why should Titania cross her Oberon?
I do but beg a little changeling boy,
To be my henchman.

   Tit.   Set your heart at rest:
The fairy land buys not the child of me.
If you will patiently dance in our round,
And see our moonlight revels, go with us;
If not, shun me, and I will spare your haunts.

   Ob. Give me that boy, and I will go with thee.

   Tit. Not for thy fairy kingdom. Fairies, away!
We shall chide downright, if I longer stay.

                        [*Exeunt* TITANIA *with her train*

   Ob. Well, go thy way: thou shalt not from this
     grove
Till I torment thee for this injury.
My gentle Puck, come hither.
Fetch me that flower; the herb I show'd thee once:
The juice of which on sleeping eyelids laid
Will make or man or woman madly dote
Upon the next live creature that it sees.
Fetch me this herb; and be thou here àgain
Ere the leviathan can swim a league.

   Puck. I'll put a girdle round about the earth
In forty minutes.   [*Exit* PUCK

   Ob.   Having once this juice,
I'll watch Titania when she is asleep,
And drop the liquor of it in her eyes.

The next thing then she waking looks upon,
She shall pursue it with the soul of love:
And ere I take this charm from off her sight,
I'll make her render up her page to me.
But who comes here? I am invisible;
And I will overhear their conference.

   Enter DEMETRIUS, HELENA *following him*

 Dem. I love thee not, therefore pursue me not.
Where is Lysander and fair Hermia?
Thou told'st me they were stolen unto this wood;
Hence, get thee gone, and follow me no more.
 Hel. You draw me, you hard-hearted adamant.
 Dem. Do I entice you? Do I speak you fair?
Or, rather, do I not in plainest truth
Tell you I do not, nor I cannot love you?
 Hel. And even for that do I love you the more.
 Dem. I'll run from thee and hide me in the
  brakes,
And leave thee to the mercy of wild beasts.
 Hel. The wildest hath not such a heart as you.
 Dem. I will not stay thy questions; let me go.
         [*Exit* DEMETRIUS
 Hel. I'll follow thee and make a heaven of hell,
To die upon the hand I love so well. [*Exit* HELENA
 Ob. Fare thee well, nymph: ere he do leave this
  grove,
Thou shalt fly him, and he shall seek thy love.

Re-enter PUCK

Hast thou the flower there? Welcome, wanderer.
 Puck. Ay, there it is.
 Ob.   I pray thee, give it me.
With juice of this I'll streak Titania's eyes,
And make her full of hateful fantasies.
Take thou some of it, and seek through this
        grove:
A sweet Athenian lady is in love
With a disdainful youth: anoint his eyes;
But do it when the next thing he espies
May be the lady: thou shalt know the man
By the Athenian garments he hath on:
And look thou meet me ere the first cock crow.
 Puck. Fear not, my lord, your servant shall do so.
                                        [*Exeunt*

Prelude

Enter TITANIA, *and her train*

 Tit. Take hands, and trip it in a round,
While I consecrate the ground.
All shall change at my command,
All shall turn to Fairyland. [1]

----

1 Here came a transformation scene to "*a Prospect of Grotto's,
Arbors, and delightful Walks*" in the original version.

3

Now, fairies, search, search everywhere,
Let no unclean thing be near,
Nothing venomous, or foul,
No raven, bat, or hooting owl,
No toad, nor elf, nor blind-worm's sting.
No poisonous herb in this place spring.
Have you search'd? Is no ill near?
   All. Nothing, nothing; all is clear.
   Tit. Let your revels now begin,
Some shall dance, and some shall sing.
All delights this place surround;
Every sweet, harmonious sound,
That e'er charm'd a skilful ear,
Meet, and entertain us here.
Let echoes plac'd in every grot
Catch and repeat each dying note.

A Fairy-⎫
Spirit. ⎭
   Come, all ye songsters of the sky,
     Wake and assemble in this wood;
   But no ill-boding bird be nigh,
     None but the harmless and the good.

Three Fairy⎫
Spirits and ⎬
Chorus. ⎭
   May the god of wit inspire
     The sacred Nine to bear a part;
   And the blessed heavenly quire
     Show the utmost of their art.
   While echo shall in sounds remote
   Repeat each note, each note, each note.

Echo

A Fairy   } *Now join your warbling voices all,*
Spirit and } *Sing, while we trip it upon the green;*
Chorus.   } *But no ill vapours rise or fall,*
            No, nothing offend our fairy queen.

This Chorus *again for a* Dance of Fairies

Tit. Come, now a roundel and a fairy song;
Then, for the third part of a minute, hence;
Some to kill cankers in the musk-rose buds,
Some war with rere-mice for their leathern wings,
To make my small elves coats, and some keep back
The clamorous owl, that nightly hoots and wonders
At our quaint spirits. Sing me now asleep;
Then to your offices and let me rest.   [*She lies down*

Enter NIGHT, MYSTERY, SECRECY, SLEEP
and their attendants

Night.   *See, even Night herself is here*
            To favour your design;
            And all her peaceful train is near
            That men to sleep incline.
            Let noise and care,
            Doubt and despair,
            Envy and spite,
            The fiend's delight,
            Be ever banish'd hence.

Let soft repose
Her eyelids close;
   And murmuring streams
   Bring pleasing dreams;
      Let nothing stay to give offence.

Mystery.   *I am come to lock all fast;*
              Love without me cannot last.
              Love, like counsels of the wise,
              Must be hid from vulgar eyes.
              'Tis holy, and we must conceal it,
              They profane it, who reveal it.

Secrecy.   *One charming night*
              Gives more delight
                Than a hundred lucky days;
              Night and I improve the taste,
              Make the pleasure longer last
                A thousand, thousand several ways.

Sleep and ⎫ *Hush, no more, be silent all;*
Chorus. ⎰   *Sweet repose has closed her eyes,*
              Soft as feather'd snow does fall!
                Softly, softly steal from hence;
                No noise disturb her sleeping sense.

A Dance *of the* Followers *of* Night

[*Exeunt* FAIRIES. TITANIA *sleeps*

Enter OBERON, *and squeezes the flower on*
TITANIA'S *eyelids*

Rondeau[1]

Ob. What thou see'st when thou dost wake,
Do it for thy true love take;
Love and languish for his sake:
Be it ounce, or cat, or bear,
Pard, or boar with bristled hair,
In thy eye that shall appear
When thou wak'st, it is thy dear:
Wake when some vile thing is near.

[*Exit* OBERON

Enter LYSANDER *and* HERMIA

Lys. Fair love, you faint with wandering in the
wood;
And to speak troth, I have forgot our way:
We'll rest us, Hermia, if you think it good,
And tarry till the comfort of the day.
Her. Be it so, Lysander: find you out a bed;
For I upon this bank will rest my head.
Lys. Here is my bed: sleep give thee all his rest.
Her. With half that wish the wisher's eyes be
press'd.   [*They sleep*

Rondeau[1]

---

1 From the *Second Music*.

Enter PUCK

Puck. Through the forest have I gone,
But Athenian found I none,
On whose eyes I might approve
This flower's force in stirring love.
Night and silence.—Who is here?
Weeds of Athens he doth wear:
This is he my master said,
Despised the Athenian maid;
And here the maiden, sleeping sound,
On the dank and dirty ground.
Churl, upon thy eyes I throw
All the power this charm doth owe.
When thou wak'st, let love forbid
Sleep his seat on thy eyelid:
So awake when I am gone;
For I must now to Oberon.   [*Exit* PUCK

A C T   III

The same. Lysander and Hermia
lying asleep

Enter DEMETRIUS *and* HELENA, *running*

Hel. Stay, though thou kill me, sweet Demetrius.
Dem. I charge thee, hence, and do not haunt me
thus.

Hel. O, wilt thou darkling leave me? do not so.
Dem. Stay, on thy peril; I alone will go.

           [*Exit* DEMETRIUS

Hel. O, I am out of breath in this fond chase!
The more my prayer, the lesser is my grace.
But who is here? Lysander! on the ground!
Dead, or asleep? I see no blood, no wound.
Lysander, if you live, good sir, awake.
   Lys. And run through fire I will for thy sweet
     sake.
Where is Demetrius? O, how fit a word
Is that vile name to perish on my sword!
   Hel. Do not say so, Lysander; say not so.
What though he love your Hermia? Lord, what
     though?
Yet Hermia still loves you; then be content.
   Lys. Content with Hermia! No, I do repent
The tedious minutes I with her have spent.
Not Hermia but Helena I love:
Who will not change a raven for a dove?
   Hel. Wherefore was I to this keen mockery born?
When at your hands did I deserve this scorn?
But fare you well: perforce I must confess
I thought you lord of more true gentleness.

           [*Exit* HELENA

   Lys. She sees not Hermia. Hermia, sleep thou
     there:

And never may'st thou come Lysander near!
And all my powers, address your love and might
To honour Helen and to be her knight!

[*Exit* LYSANDER

Her. (*awaking*). Help me, Lysander, help me! do
　　thy best
To pluck this crawling serpent from my breast!
Ay me, for pity! what a dream was here!
Lysander, look how I do quake with fear:
Methought a serpent eat my heart away,
And you sat smiling at his cruel prey.
Lysander! what, removed? Lysander! lord!
What, out of hearing? gone? no sound, no word?
Alack, where are you? speak, an if you hear;
Speak, of all loves; I swoon almost with fear.
No?—then I well perceive you are not nigh:
Either death or you I'll find immediately.

[*Exit* HERMIA

Enter QUINCE, SNUG, BOTTOM, FLUTE, SNOUT
and STARVELING

Bot. Are we all met?

Qui. Pat, pat; and here's a marvellous con-
venient place for our rehearsal. This green plot
shall be our stage and we will do it in action as
we will do it before the duke.

Enter PUCK *behind*

    Puck. What hempen homespuns have we swag-
      gering here,
So near the cradle of the fairy queen?
What! a play toward; I'll be an auditor;
An actor too perhaps, if I see cause.
    Prologue. If we offend, it is with our good will.
    That you should think we come not to offend,
But with good will. To show our simple skill,
    That is the true beginning of our end.
Consider then we come but in despite.
    We do not come as minding to content you,
Our true intent is. All for your delight
    We are not here. That you should here repent
      you,
The actors are at hand and by their show
You shall know all that you are like to know.
Gentles, perchance you wonder at this show;
    But wonder on, till truth make all things plain.
This man is Pyramus, if you would know;
    This beauteous lady Thisby is certain.
This man, with lime and rough-cast, doth present
    Wall, that vile Wall which did these lovers
      sunder:
And through Wall's chink, poor souls, they are
      content

4

To whisper. At the which let no man wonder.
This man, with lanthorn, dog, and bush of thorn,
   Presenteth Moonshine: for, if you will know,
By moonshine did these lovers think no scorn
   To meet at Ninus' tomb, there, there to woo.
This grisly beast, which Lion hight by name,
The trusty Thisby, coming first by night,
Did scare away, or rather did affright;
And, as she fled, her mantle she did fall,
   Which Lion vile with bloody mouth did stain.
Anon comes Pyramus, sweet youth and tall,
   And finds his trusty Thisby's mantle slain:
Whereat, with blade, with bloody blameful blade,
   He bravely broach'd his boiling bloody breast;
And Thisby, tarrying in mulberry shade,
   His dagger drew, and died. For all the rest,
Let Lion, Moonshine, Wall, and lovers twain
At large discourse, while here they do remain.
   Wall. In this same interlude it doth befall
That I, one Snout by name, present a wall;
And such a wall, as I would have you think,
That had in it a crannied hole or chink,
Through which the lovers, Pyramus and Thisby,
Did whisper often very secretly.
This loam, this rough-cast and this stone doth
      show
That I am that same wall; the truth is so:

And this the cranny is, right and sinister,
Through which the fearful lovers are to whisper.
    Pyr. O grim-look'd night! O night with hue
      so black!
    O night, which ever art when day is not!
O night, O night! alack, alack, alack,
    I fear my Thisby's promise is forgot!
And thou, O wall, O sweet, O lovely wall,
    That stands between her father's ground and
      mine!
Thou wall, O wall, O sweet and lovely wall,
    Show me thy chink, to blink through with mine
      eyne!   [WALL *holds up his fingers*
Thanks, courteous wall: Jove shield thee well for
    this!
    But what see I? No Thisby do I see.
O wicked wall, through whom I see no bliss!
    Cursed be thy stones for thus deceiving me!
    Thi. O wall, full often hast thou heard my moans,
    For parting my fair Pyramus and me!
My cherry lips have often kiss'd thy stones,
    Thy stones with lime and hair knit up in thee.
    Pyr. I see a voice: now will I to the chink,
    To spy an I can hear my Thisby's face.
Thisby!
    Thi. My love thou art, my love I think.
    Pyr. Think what thou wilt, I am thy lover's grace;

And like Limander, am I trusty still.

   Thi. And I like Helen, till the Fates me kill.

   Pyr. Not Shafalus to Procrus was so true.

   Thi. As Shafalus to Procrus, I to you.

   Pyr. O, kiss me through the hole of this vile wall!

   Thi. I kiss the wall's hole, not your lips at all.

   Pyr. Wilt thou at Ninny's tomb meet me straightway?

   Thi. 'Tide life, 'tide death, I come without delay.

   Wall. Thus have I, Wall, my part discharged so;

And, being done, thus Wall away doth go.

   Lion. You, ladies, you, whose gentle hearts do fear

The smallest monstrous mouse that creeps on floor,

May now perchance both quake and tremble here,

   When lion rough in wildest rage doth roar.

Then know that I, one Snug the joiner, am

A lion-fell, nor else no lion's dam;

For, if I should as lion come in strife

Into this place, 'twere pity on my life.

   Moonshine. This lanthorn doth the horned moon present;

Myself the man i' the moon do seem to be.

   All that I have to say, is, to tell you that the lanthorn is the moon; I, the man in the moon; this

thorn-bush, my thorn-bush; and this dog, my
dog.

   Thi. This is old Ninny's tomb. Where is my
     love?

   Lion (roaring). Oh—   [THISBE *runs off*

   Pyr. Sweet Moon, I thank thee for thy sunny
     beams;

I thank thee, Moon, for shining now so bright;

For, by thy gracious, golden, glittering gleams,

   I trust to take of truest Thisby sight.

        But stay, O spite!

        But mark, poor knight,

          What dreadful dole is here!

        Eyes, do you see?

        How can it be?

          O dainty duck! O dear!

        Thy mantle good,

        What, stain'd with blood!

          Approach, ye Furies fell!

        O Fates, come, come,

        Cut thread and thrum;

          Quail, crush, conclude, and quell!

O wherefore, Nature, didst thou lions frame?

   Since lion vile hath here deflower'd my dear:

Which is—no, no—which was the fairest dame

   That lived, that loved, that liked, that look'd
     with cheer.

Come, tears, confound;
Out, sword, and wound
　　The pap of Pyramus;
Ay, that left pap,
Where heart doth hop:　　　　*[Stabs himself*
　　Thus die I, thus, thus, thus.
Now am I dead,
Now am I fled;
　　My soul is in the sky:
Tongue, lose thy light;
Moon, take thy flight:
　　Now die, die, die, die, die.　　　*[Dies*

Thi. Asleep, my love?
What, dead, my dove?
　　O Pyramus, arise!
Speak, speak. Quite dumb?
Dead, dead? A tomb
　　Must cover thy sweet eyes.
These lily lips,
This cherry nose,
　　These yellow cowslip cheeks,
Are gone, are gone:
Lovers, make moan:
　　His eyes were green as leeks.
O Sisters Three,
Come, come to me,
　　With hands as pale as milk;

Lay them in gore,
Since you have shore
   With shears his thread of silk.
Tongue, not a word:
Come, trusty sword;
   Come, blade, my breast imbrue:

                              [*Stabs herself*

And, farewell, friends;
Thus Thisby ends:
   Adieu, adieu, adieu.   [*Dies*

Sno. Come, get up, Pyramus and Thisbe, and let
me speak the Epilogue.

Puck. No, no, I'll be the Epilogue.

Qui. O monstrous! O strange! we are haunted.
Pray, masters! fly, masters! help!

            [*Exeunt* QUINCE, SNUG, FLUTE, SNOUT
                  and STARVELING

Puck. I'll follow you, I'll lead you about a round,
   Through bog, through bush, through brake,
      through brier:
Sometime a horse I'll be, sometime a hound,
   A hog, a headless bear, sometime a fire:
      And neigh, and bark, and grunt, and roar, and
         burn,
      Like horse, hound, hog, bear, fire, at every
         turn.   [*Exit* PUCK

Bot. (*with an ass's head*). Why do they run away?

this is a knavery of them to make me afeard. But
I will not stir from this place, do what they can:
I will walk up and down here, and I will sing, that
they shall hear I am not afraid.   [*Sings*

>   The ousel-cock, so black of hue,
>   With orange-tawny bill,
>   The throstle with his note so true,
>   The wren with little quill.

Tit. (*awaking*). What angel wakes me from my
   flowery bed?

Bot. (*sings*).

>   The finch, the sparrow, and the lark,
>   The plain-song cuckoo gray,
>   Whose note full many a man doth mark,
>   And dares not answer, nay.

Tit. I pray thee, gentle mortal, sing again:
Mine ear is much enamour'd of thy note;
So is mine eye enthralled to thy shape;
And thy fair virtue's force perforce doth move me,
On the first view, to say, to swear, I love thee.

Bot. Methinks, mistress, you should have little
reason for that: and yet, to say the truth, reason
and love keep little company together now-a-days.

Tit. Thou art as wise as thou art beautiful.

Bot. Not so, neither; but if I had wit enough to
get out of this wood, I have enough to serve mine
own turn.

Tit. Out of this wood do not desire to go:
Thou shalt remain here, whether thou wilt or no:
And I do love thee: therefore, go with me;
I'll give thee fairies to attend on thee.
Come, sit thee down upon this flowery bed,
　While I thy amiable cheeks do coy,
And stick musk-roses in thy sleek smooth head,
　And kiss thy fair large ears, my gentle joy.
What, wilt thou hear some music, my sweet love?

Bot. I have a reasonable good ear in music.
Let's have the tongs and bones.

Tit. Away, my elves; prepare a fairy mask
To entertain my love; and change this place
To my enchanted lake. [1]

Prelude

Enter a troop of FAWNS, DRYADS *and* NAIADS

(A Dryad) and Chorus.

If love's a sweet passion, why does it torment?
If a bitter, oh tell me whence comes my content?
Since I suffer with pleasure, why should I complain?
Or grieve at my fate, when I know 'tis in vain?

---

1 Here came a transformation scene to a great wood, with
a river—spanned by a dragon-bridge—in the middle, on
which two swans were swimming.

*Yet so pleasing the pain is, so soft is
the dart,*

*That at once it both wounds me and
tickles my heart.*

*I press her hand gently, look languishing
down,*

*And by passionate silence I make my
love known.*

*But oh! how I'm blest when so kind she
does prove*

*By some willing mistake to discover her
love,*

*When in striving to hide, she reveals
all her flame,*

*And our eyes tell each other what neither
dares name.*

While a symphony is playing, the two SWANS *come swimming on
to the bank of the river, as if they would land; these turn themselves
into* FAIRIES *and dance.*[1]

Four SAVAGES *enter, fright the* FAIRIES *away,
and dance an entry*[2]

---

1 A reduction of the original stage-direction.
2 In the 1693 version a bravura song for a soprano, "Ye
gentle spirits of the air", was interpolated here.

Enter CORIDON *and* MOPSA

Cor.   *Now the maids and the men are making of*
       hay,
    We've left the dull fools and are stolen
       away.
     Then, Mopsa, no more
     Be coy as before,
    But let us merrily, merrily play,
    And kiss and kiss the sweet time away.

Mop. *Why how now, Sir Clown, what makes you*
       so bold?
    I'd have you to know I'm not made of that
       mould.
     I tell you again,
     Maids must kiss no men.
    No, no; no, no; no kissing at all.
    I'll not kiss till I kiss you for good and
       all.

Cor.   *Should you give me a score,*
    'Twould not lessen your store;
    Then bid me cheerfully, cheerfully kiss,
    And take, and take my fill of your bliss.

Mop. *I'll not trust you so far, I know you too*
       well:
    Should I give you an inch, you'd soon take
       an ell.

          Then lordlike you rule,
          And laugh at the fool.
          No, no; no, no; no kissing at all.
          I'll not kiss till I kiss you for good and all.
Cor.   *So small a request you must not deny,*
          Nor will I admit of another reply.
Mop.   *Nay! what do you mean? Oh fie, fie, fie, fie!*
A Nymph. *When I have often heard young maids*
               complaining
             That, when men promise most, they
               most deceive,
          Then I thought none of them worthy my
             gaining,
             And what they swore resolv'd ne'er to
               believe.
          But, when so humbly he made his addresses,
             With looks so soft and with language so
               kind,
          I thought it sin to refuse his caresses;
             Nature o'ercame and I soon chang'd my
               mind.
          Should he employ all his wit in deceiving,
             Stretch his invention and artfully feign;
          I find such charms, such true joy in be-
               lieving,
             I'll have the pleasure, let him have the
               pain.

If he proves perjur'd, I shall not be cheated;
He may deceive himself, but never me;
'Tis what I look for, and shan't be defeated,
For I'll be as false and inconstant as he.

A Dance *of* Haymakers

(A Nymph) ⎫ *A thousand, thousand ways we'll find*
and Chorus. ⎭   *To entertain the hours;*
                No two shall e'er be known so kind,
                No life so blest as ours.

INTERVAL

ACT IV

Air[1]

The same. Titania and Bottom asleep

Enter OBERON

Ob. I wonder if Titania be awak'd;
Then, what it was that next came in her eye,
Here comes my messenger.

---

1 The *Fourth Act Tune.*

Enter PUCK

How now, mad spirit!
What night-rule now about this haunted grove?
  Puck. My mistress with a monster is in love.
Near to her close and consecrated bower,
While she was in her dull and sleeping hour,
A crew of patches, rude mechanicals,
That work for bread upon Athenian stalls,
Were met together to rehearse a play
Intended for great Theseus' nuptial-day.
The shallowest thick-skin of that barren sort,
Who Pyramus presented in their sport,
Forsook his scene and enter'd in a brake:
When I did him at this advantage take,
An ass's nole I fixed on his head:
Anon his Thisbe must be answered,
And forth my mimic comes. When they him spy,
Straight at his sight away his fellows fly.
I led them on in this distracted fear,
And left sweet Pyramus translated there;
When in that moment, so it came to pass,
Titania wak'd and straightway lov'd an ass.
  Ob. This falls out better than I could devise.
But hast thou yet latch'd the Athenian's eyes
With the love-juice, as I did bid thee do?
  Puck. I took him sleeping—that is finished too—

And the Athenian woman by his side;
That, when he wak'd, of force she must be ey'd.

Enter DEMETRIUS *and* HERMIA

Ob. Stand close; this is the same Athenian.
Puck. This is the woman, but not this the
  man.

Dem. O, why rebuke you him that loves you so?
Lay breath so bitter on your bitter foe.

Her. If thou hast slain Lysander in his sleep,
Being o'er shoes in blood, plunge in the deep,
And kill me too.

Dem. You spend your passion on a misprised
  mood:
I am not guilty of Lysander's blood;
Nor is he dead, for aught that I can tell.

Her. I pray thee, tell me then that he is well.

Dem. An if I could, what should I get therefore?

Her. A privilege never to see me more.
And from thy hated presence part I so:
See me no more, whether he be dead or no.

[*Exit* HERMIA

Dem. There is no following her in this fierce
  vein:
Here therefore for a while I will remain.
So sorrow's heaviness doth heavier grow
For debt that bankrupt sleep doth sorrow owe;

Which now in some slight measure it will pay,
If for his tender here I make some stay.

[Lies down and sleeps [1]

   Ob. What hast thou done? Thou hast mistaken
     quite,
And laid the love-juice on some true-love's sight
About the wood go swifter than the wind,
And Helena of Athens look thou find:
By some illusion see thou bring her here:
I'll charm his eyes against she do appear.
   Puck. I go, I go; look how I go,
Swifter than arrow from the Tartar's bow.

[Exit PUCK [2]

Rondeau [3]

   Ob. Flower of this purple dye, [4]
      Hit with Cupid's archery,

[Squeezes the flower on DEMETRIUS' *eyelids*

      Sink in apple of his eye.
      When his love he doth espy,
      Let her shine as gloriously
      As the Venus of the sky.

---

1 In the original Demetrius and Hermia only cross the stage.
2 In the original Titania's entertainment for Bottom took place here.
3 From the *Second Music*.
4 The beginning of Act IV in the original version.

When thou wak'st, if she be by,
Beg of her for remedy.

Enter PUCK

Puck. Captain of our fairy band,
Helena is here at hand;
And the youth, mistook by me,
Pleading for a lover's fee.
Shall we their fond pageant see?
Lord, what fools these mortals be!

Enter LYSANDER *and* HELENA

Lys. Why should you think that I should woo
in scorn?
Scorn and derision never come in tears:
Look, when I vow, I weep; and vows so born,
In their nativity all truth appears.
Hel. You do advance your cunning more and
more.
When truth kills truth, O devilish-holy fray!
These vows are Hermia's: will you give her o'er?
Weigh oath with oath, and you will nothing
weigh.
Lys. Demetrius loves her, and he loves not you.
Dem. (*awaking*). O Helen, goddess, nymph, per-
fect, divine!
To what, my love, shall I compare thine eyne?

6

Crystal is muddy. O, how ripe in show
Thy lips, those kissing cherries, tempting grow!

Hel. O spite! O hell! I see you all are bent
To set against me for your merriment.

Lys. You are unkind, Demetrius; be not so;
For you love Hermia: this, you know, I know.

Dem. Lysander, keep thy Hermia; I will none:
If e'er I lov'd her, all that love is gone.
Look, where thy love comes; yonder is thy dear.

Enter HERMIA

Her. Thou art not by mine eye, Lysander, found;
Mine ear, I thank it, brought me to thy sound.
But why unkindly didst thou leave me so?

    Lys. Why should he stay, whom love doth press
        to go?

    Her. What love could press Lysander from my
        side?

    Lys. Lysander's love, that would not let him
        bide,

Fair Helena, who more engilds the night
Than all yon fiery oes and eyes of light.

    Her. You speak not as you think: it cannot
        be.

Hel. Lo, she is one of this confederacy!
But fare ye well: 'tis partly my own fault,
Which death or absence soon shall remedy.

Lys. Stay, gentle Helena; hear my excuse:
My love, my life, my soul, fair Helena!

Her. O me! you juggler! you canker-blossom!
You thief of love! what, have you come by night
And stolen my love's heart from him?

Hel.   Fine, i'faith!
Fie, fie! you counterfeit, you puppet, you!

Her. Puppet? why so? ay, that way goes the
    game.
And are you grown so high in his esteem,
Because I am so dwarfish and so low?
How low am I, thou painted maypole? speak:
How low am I? I am not yet so low
But that my nails can reach unto thine eyes.

Lys. Be not afraid; she shall not harm thee,
    Helena.

Dem. No, sir, she shall not, though you take
    her part.

Hel. O, when she's angry, she is keen and
    shrewd:
And, though she be but little, she is fierce.

Her. Little again? nothing but low and little?
Let me come to her.

Lys.   Get you gone, you dwarf,
You bead, you acorn. Now she holds me not;
Now follow, if thou dar'st, to try whose right,
Of thine or mine, is most in Helena.

Dem. Follow! nay, I'll go with thee, cheek by
     jole.   [*Exeunt* LYSANDER *and* DEMETRIUS
Her. You, mistress, all this coil is 'long of you:
Nay, go not back.
    Hel.   I will not trust you, I;
Your hands than mine are quicker for a fray,
My legs are longer though, to run away.
          [*Exit* HELENA *running and* HERMIA *after her*
    Ob. This is thy negligence: still thou mistak'st,
Or else committ'st thy knaveries wilfully.
    Puck. Believe me, king of shadows, I mistook.
    Ob. Thou see'st these lovers seek a place to fight:
Hie therefore, Robin, overcast the night;
And lead these testy rivals so astray
As one comes not within another's way,
Till o'er their brows death-counterfeiting sleep
With leaden legs and batty wings doth creep.
Whiles I in this affair do thee employ,
I'll to my queen and beg her Indian boy;
And then I will her charmed eye release
From monster's view, and all things shall be peace.
          [*Exit* OBERON
    Puck. Up and down, up and down,
        I will lead them up and down:
        I am fear'd in field and town:
        Goblin, lead them up and down.
Here comes one.

Re-enter LYSANDER

Lys. Where art thou, proud Demetrius? speak
  thou now.

Puck. Here, villain; drawn and ready. Where art
  thou?

Lys. I will be with thee straight.

Puck.   Follow me, then,
To plainer ground.
                            [*Exit* LYSANDER, *as following the voice*

Re-enter DEMETRIUS

Dem. Lysander! speak again:
Thou runaway, thou coward, art thou fled?
Speak! In some bush? Where dost thou hide thy
  head?

Puck. Thou coward, art thou bragging to the
  stars,
Telling the bushes that thou look'st for wars,
And wilt not come? Come recreant.

Dem.   Art thou there?

Puck. Follow my voice: we'll try no manhood
  here.   [*Exeunt*

Re-enter LYSANDER

Lys. The villain is much lighter-heel'd than I:
I follow'd fast, but faster he did fly;
That fallen am I in dark uneven way,
And here will rest me. Come, thou gentle day!
                                          [*Lies down*

For if but once thou show me thy grey light,
I'll find Demetrius and revenge this spite.   [*Sleeps*

Re-enter PUCK *and* DEMETRIUS

Puck. Ho, ho, ho! Coward, why com'st thou
    not?
Dem. Abide me, if thou dar'st; for well I wot
Thou runn'st before me, shifting every place,
And dar'st not stand, nor look me in the face.
Where art thou now?
Puck.   Come hither: I am here.
Dem. Nay, then, thou mock'st me. Thou shalt
    buy this dear,
If ever I thy face by daylight see:
Now, go thy way. Faintness constraineth me
To measure out my length on this cold bed.
By day's approach look to be visited.

                              [*Lies down and sleeps*

Re-enter HELENA

Hel. O weary night, O long and tedious night,
    Abate thy hours! Shine comforts from the east,
That I may back to Athens by daylight,
    From these that my poor company detest:
And sleep, that sometimes shuts up sorrow's eye,
Steal me awhile from mine own company.
                              [*Lies down and sleeps*
    Puck. Yet but three? Come one more;

Two of both kinds makes up four.
Here she comes, curst and sad:
Cupid is a knavish lad,
Thus to make poor females mad.

Re-enter HERMIA

Her. Never so weary, never so in woe,
  Bedabbled with the dew, and torn with briers,
I can no further crawl, no further go;
  My legs can keep no pace with my desires.
Here will I rest me till the break of day.
Heavens shield Lysander, if they mean a fray.
                              [*Lies down and sleeps*

Enter OBERON

Ob. Thou hast perform'd exactly each command.
Titania too has given me the sweet boy.
And now I have him, I will straight undo
This hateful imperfection of her eyes:

Rondeau[1]

Be as thou wast wont to be;
                    [*Touching her eyes with an herb*
See as thou wast wont to see:
Dian's bud o'er Cupid's flower
Hath such force and blessed power.
Now, my Titania; wake you, my sweet queen.

___

1 From the *Second Music.*

Tit. My Oberon! what visions have I seen!
Methought I was enamour'd of an ass.

    Ob. There lies your love.

    Tit.   How came these things to pass?
O, how mine eyes do loathe his visage now!

    Ob. Silence awhile. Robin, take off this head.

    Puck. Now, when thou wak'st, with thine own
       fool's eyes peep.

    Ob. Titania, call for music.

    Tit. Let us have all variety of music,
All that should welcome up the rising sun. [1]

Symphony

The FOUR SEASONS *enter, with their several attendants*

An Attendant and Chorus.	*Now the night is chas'd away,* *All salute the rising sun;* *'Tis the happy, happy day,* *The birthday of King Oberon.*
Two Attendants.	*Let the fifes and the clarions and shrill trumpets sound,* *And the arch of high heaven the clangor resound.*

---

[1] In the original the scene changed to a *Garden of Fountains*.

Entry of Phoebus

Phoebus. *When a cruel long winter has frozen the earth,*
And nature imprison'd seeks in vain to be
free,
I dart forth my beams, to give all things a birth,
Making spring for the plants, every flower
and each tree.
'Tis I who give life, warmth, and vigour to all,
Ev'n love, who rules all things in earth, air
and sea,
Would languish and fade, and to nothing
would fall,
The world to its chaos would return but
for me.

Chorus. *Hail! great parent of us all,*
Light and comfort of the earth:
Before your shrine the seasons fall,
Thou who giv'st all nature birth.

Spring. *Thus the ever grateful Spring*
Does her yearly tribute bring;
All your sweets before him lay,
Then round his altar sing and play.

Summer. *Here's the Summer, sprightly, gay,*
Smiling, wanton, fresh and fair,
Adorn'd with all the flowers of May,
Whose various sweets perfume the air.

7

Autumn. *See, my many-coloured fields*
  And loaded trees my will obey;
  All the fruit that Autumn yields
  I offer to the God of Day.

Winter. *Now Winter comes slowly, pale, meagre and*
    old,
  First trembling with age and then quiv'ring
    with cold;
  Benumb'd with hard frosts and with snow
    cover'd o'er,
  Prays the Sun to restore him and sings as
    before.

Chorus. *Hail! great parent of us all,*
  Before your shrine the seasons fall,
    Thou who giv'st all nature birth.

A Dance *of the* Four Seasons [1]

  Ob. Now, my Puck, this herb apply
To the mistaken lover's eye;
The powerful juice will clear his sight
Make 'em friends and set all right.

  Tit. Come, my lord; and in our flight
Tell me how it came this night
That I sleeping here was found
With these mortals on the ground.

                            [*Exeunt all but* PUCK

---
1 The *Air* (Appendix IV) in the Purcell Society Edition of
The Fairy Queen.

Rondeau[1]

Puck. On the ground
   Sleep sound:
   I'll apply
   To your eye,
     Gentle lover, remedy.
                    [*Squeezing the juice on* LYSANDER'S *eyes*
   When thou wak'st,
   Thou tak'st
   True delight
   In the sight
     Of thy former lady's eye;
   And the country proverb known,
   That every man should take his own,
   In your waking shall be shown:
     Jack shall have Jill;
     Nought shall go ill;
       The man shall have his mare again,
         And all shall be well.   [*Exit* PUCK

---

1 From the *Second Music.*

ACT V : SCENE I

The same

Symphony[1]

Enter THESEUS, EGEUS *and train*

The. Go, one of you, find out the forester;
I long to hear the music of my hounds;
Uncouple in the western valley; let them go.
But soft, what nymphs are these?

Eg. My lord, this is my daughter here asleep;
And this, Lysander; this Demetrius is;
This Helena, old Nedar's Helena;
I wonder of their being here together.

    The. Go, bid the huntsmen wake them with
      their music.

LYSANDER, DEMETRIUS, HELENA *and* HERMIA
awake and start up

Good morrow, friends. Saint Valentine is past:
Begin these wood-birds but to couple now?

    Lys. Pardon, my lord.

    The.   I pray you all, stand up.
I know you two are rival enemies:
How comes this gentle concord in the world,
That hatred is so far from jealousy,
To sleep by hate, and fear no enmity?

---

1 The *Symphony* to "Thus the gloomy world".

Lys. My lord, I shall reply amazedly,
Half sleep, half waking: but as yet, I swear,
I cannot truly say how I came here;
But, as I think—for truly would I speak,
I came with Hermia hither: our intent
Was to be gone from Athens, where we might
Without the peril of the Athenian law—
    Eg. Enough, enough, my lord; you have
        enough:
I beg the law, the law, upon his head.
They would have stolen away; they would,
        Demetrius,
Thereby to have defeated you and me.
    Dem. My lord, fair Helen told me of their
        stealth,
And I in fury hither follow'd them,
Fair Helena in fancy following me.
But, my good lord, I wot not by what power—
But by some power it is—my love to Hermia,
Melted as the snow, seems to me now
As the remembrance of an idle gaud,
Which in my childhood I did dote upon;
And all the faith, the virtue of my heart,
The object and the pleasure of mine eye,
Is only Helena.
    The. Fair lovers, you are fortunately met;
Of this discourse we more will hear anon.

Egeus, I will be a father too,
And give fair Helen to Demetrius.
Then feast these lovers royally; away.   [*Exeunt all*

Symphony[1]

Bot. (*awaking*). When my cue comes, call me, and I will answer: my next is, "Most fair Pyramus". Heigh-ho! Peter Quince! Flute, the bellows-mender! Snout, the tinker! Starveling! God's my life, stolen hence, and left me asleep! I have had a most rare vision. I have had a dream, past the wit of man to say what dream it was: man is but an ass, if he go about to expound this dream. Methought I was—there is no man can tell what. Methought I was—and methought I had—but man is but a patched fool, if he will offer to say what methought I had. I will get Peter Quince to write a ballad of this dream, and I will sing it in the latter end of a play, before the duke.   [*Exit* BOTTOM

Hornpipe[2]

---

1 *v. supra.*
2 The *Third Act Tune.*

SCENE II

Quince's House

Enter QUINCE, FLUTE, SNOUT *and* STARVELING

Qui. Have you sent to Bottom's house? is he come home yet?

Sta. He cannot be heard of. Out of doubt he is transported.

Flu. If he come not, then the play is marred: it goes not forward, doth it?

Qui. It is not possible: you have not a man in all Athens able to discharge Pyramus but he.

Flu. No, he hath simply the best wit of any handicraft man in Athens.

Qui. Yea, and the best person too; and he is a very paramour for a sweet voice.

Flu. You must say "paragon": a paramour is, God bless us, a thing of naught.

Enter SNUG

Snu. Masters, the duke is coming from the temple, and there is two or three lords and ladies more married: if our sport had gone forward, we had all been made men.

Flu. O sweet bully Bottom! Thus hath he lost sixpence a day during his life: he could not have 'scaped sixpence a day: an the duke had not given him sixpence a day for playing Pyramus, I'll be hanged; he would have deserved it: sixpence a day in Pyramus, or nothing.

Enter BOTTOM

Bot. Where are these lads? where are these hearts?

Qui. Bottom! O most courageous day! O most happy hour!

Bot. Masters, I am to discourse wonders: but ask me not what: for if I tell you, I am no true Athenian. I will tell you every thing, right as it fell out.

Qui. Let us hear, sweet Bottom.

Bot. Not a word of me. All that I will tell you is, that the duke hath dined. Get your apparel together, good strings to your beards, new ribbons to your pumps; meet presently at the palace; every man look o'er his part; for the short and the long is, our play is preferr'd. In any case, let Thisby have clean linen; and let not him that plays the lion pare his nails, for they shall hang out for the lion's claws. And, most dear actors, eat no onions nor garlic, for we are to utter sweet breath; and I do not doubt but to hear them say, it is a sweet comedy. No more words: away! go, away!

[*Exeunt*

Entry Dance

SCENE III

The Palace of Theseus

Enter THESEUS, EGEUS, HERMIA, HELENA, LYSANDER,
DEMETRIUS, Q'UINCE, FLUTE, SNUG, SNOUT,
STARVELING *and* BOTTOM

Eg. Are not these stories strange, my gracious
    lord?

The. More strange than true: I never may believe
These antique fables, nor these fairy toys.
Lovers and madmen have such seething brains,
Such shaping fantasies, that apprehend
More than cool reason ever comprehends.

Air[1]

Enter OBERON, TITANIA, PUCK *and all the fairies*

I hear strange music warbling in the air.

Ob. 'Tis fairy music, sent by me
To cure your incredulity.
All was true the lovers told,
You shall stranger things behold.

Tit. Sir, then cast your eyes above;
See the wife of mighty Jove.

---

1 The *Second Act Tune.*

8

Prelude *to the* Epithalamium

Ob. Juno, who does still preside
O'er the sacred nuptial bed,
Comes to bless their days and nights
With all true joys and chaste delights.

Juno. *Thrice happy lovers, may you be*
For ever, ever free
From that tormenting devil, jealousy,
From all the anxious cares and strife
That attends a married life:
Be to one another true,
Kind to her as she's to you;
And since the errors of the night are past,
May he be ever constant, she be ever chaste.[1]

Ob. Now let a new transparent world be seen,
All nature join to entertain our queen.
Now we are reconcil'd, all things agree
To make an universal harmony.

The scene changes to a Chinese Garden

A Chinese ⎫ *Thus, thus the gloomy world*
Man.   ⎬   *At first began to shine,*
         ⎭   *And from the power divine*

---

1 At this point in the 1693 version *The Plaint* was interpolated.

A glory round it hurl'd,
  Which made it bright,
    And gave it birth in light.

Then were all minds as pure
  As those ethereal streams,
In innocence secure,
  Not subject to extremes.
    There was no room then for empty
      fame,
    No cause for pride, ambition wanted
      aim.

A Chinese⎫ *Thus happy and free,*
Woman. ⎭ *Thus treated are we*
    With Nature's chiefest delights;
We never cloy,
But renew our joy,
  And one bliss another invites.

Chorus.   *Thus wildly we live,*
Thus freely we give
    What Heaven as freely bestows;
We were not made
For labour or trade,
  Which fools on each other impose.

A Chinese⎫ *Yes, Xansi, in your looks I find*
Man. ⎭   *The charms by which my heart's be-*
      tray'd;

Then let not your disdain unbind
The prisoner that your eyes have made.
She that in love makes least defence
Wounds ever with the surest dart;
Beauty may captivate the sense,
But kindness only gains the heart.

Six MONKEYS *come from between the trees and dance*

First Woman. *Hark how all things in one sound rejoice,*
And the world seems to have one voice.

Second Woman. *Hark! hark! the ech'ing air a triumph sings,*
And all around pleas'd Cupids clap their wings.

Chorus. *Hark! Hark! Hark!*

Second Woman. *Sure the dull God of Marriage does not hear.*

Both Women. *We'll rouse him with a charm. Hymen, appear!*

Chorus. *Hymen, appear!*

Both Women and Chorus. *Our Queen of Night commands thee not to stay.*

Prelude

Enter HYMEN

Hymen.
> *See, see I obey,*
> *My torch has long been out; I hate*
> *On loose dissembling vows to wait,*
> > *Where hardly love outlives the*
> > *wedding night.*
> > *False flames, love's meteors, yield*
> > *my torch no light.* [1]

Both Women.
> *Turn then thine eyes upon those glories*
> *here,*
> *And catching flames will on thy torch*
> *appear.*

Hymen.
> *My torch indeed will from such*
> *brightness shine.*
> *Love ne'er had yet such altars so*
> *divine.*

The Grand Dance *begins*

---

[1] A further transformation took place here in the original version.

Hymen,   *They shall be as happy as they're fair;*
Both Women }   *Love shall fill all the places of care;*
and Chorus.   *And every time the sun shall display*
                          His rising light,
                     It shall be to them a new wedding-day,
                          And when he sets a new nuptial
                               night.

Chaconne

T H E   E N D

Printed in the United States
By Bookmasters